The
Fortunate
Fortunes

The Fortunate Fortunes

by Nathan Aaseng

Lerner Publications Company
Minneapolis

Page two: A worker at the Johnson Wax Company inspects cans of wax as they travel along the assembly line.

Library of Congress Cataloging-in-Publication Data

Aaseng, Nathan.
  The fortunate fortunes / by Nathan Aaseng.
    p.   cm.
  Includes index.
  Summary: Recounts the success stories of entrepreneurs who were able to found profitable companies or make lucrative developments through a combination of imagination and luck.
  ISBN 0-8225-0678-5
  1. Businessmen—Biography—Juvenile literature. 2. Success in business—Juvenile literature. 3. Creative ability in business —Juvenile literature. [1. Businessmen. 2. Business enterprises.] I. Title.
HC29.A235   1989
338'.04'0922—dc19
[B]
[920]   88-3025
                                                               CIP
                                                                AC

Manufactured in the United States of America

1 2 3 4 5 6 7 8 9 10 99 98 97 96 95 94 93 92 91 90 89

To Kelli

Contents

A lucky train ride in 1930 led to the creation of Bisquick, the first ready-mixed baking blend. Today Bisquick is still one of the most popular baking mixes.

Introduction

WHAT DOES IT TAKE TO BLAZE A TRAIL
of success through the intimidating world of business? How do you take an idea or a new product or
an invention and brand it into the public's memory?

Success in business requires many ingredients—
some obvious, others less so. Hard work, innovation,
creativity, enthusiasm, sales ability, wise management, courage, and the ability to spot trends in
society all contribute to success.

The dictionary defines an entrepreneur as "one
who organizes, manages, and *assumes the risks* of
a business." If it were simply a matter of following
the right plan and working hard, everyone could be
an entrepreneur and start a successful business. But
business is a gamble, and even businesses that have
the right ingredients fail. Somewhere along the way,

companies need something else to give them an extra push. This key ingredient is luck.

In the history of many companies is a stroke of luck that someone saw as an opportunity to be seized. In 1930 Carl Smith, a sales executive working for General Mills, boarded a train in Portland, Oregon. By the time he reached the dining car, it was well past the usual lunch hour. Expecting a meal of warmed leftovers, he was surprised to receive fresh, hot biscuits within 15 minutes.

Baffled, Smith went back to talk with the chef, who revealed his secret. Before leaving Portland, the chef had blended a mixture of flour, lard, baking powder, and salt, which he stored in an ice chest. When someone ordered fresh biscuits, he could make them quickly, without any measuring or mixing.

Smith reported his experience to others at General Mills. Taking the chef's lead, the company came out with Bisquick, a ready-mixed baking blend. It proved so popular that 96 imitation products appeared on the market within a year. By being the first, Bisquick became the leading brand and remains popular to this day. Smith's lucky train ride led to the creation of a successful product.

In the 1850s, a guest at Moon's Lake House in Sarasota Springs, New York, sent his fried potatoes back to the kitchen several times. They weren't "properly thin," he claimed. After several attempts to please the dissatisfied diner, chef George Crum decided he'd been pushed too far. Angrily, he sliced

An 1870s "Saratoga Chips" box features Moon's Lake House, where the potato chip was born in the 1850s.

a potato paper-thin, fried the slices, and sarcastically offered them to the guest. Instead of feeling insulted, the man proclaimed the potato chips delicious.

By trying to spite a finicky guest, the chef had invented the potato chip. Soon Crum's Saratoga Chips were in great demand, and potato chips have remained a favorite snack ever since.

These brief stories illustrate some ways that luck can affect the business world. The stories that follow take a more detailed look at the role of luck in creating some of the most popular products and best-known businesses.

We will discover that Charles Hires happened to be in the right place at the right time and turned his opportunity into a fortune. We will see how products such as Kleenex tissue, fiberglass, and Wrigley's gum were stumbled onto by accident. Finally, we will see how Will Keith Kellogg's blunder made him a millionaire.

Of course, business success is not just a matter of luck. Small opportunities can be overlooked and even the greatest strokes of luck can be wasted. This book tells the stories of those who got a break and took advantage of it to create a lasting impact on the marketplace.

At least we agree on Hires

A Pure Delicious Beverage for the HOME
IN BOTTLES *or* AT FOUNTAINS

Hires's Honeymoon

Hires Root Beer

According to a popular saying, "it's better to be lucky than good." But as most people know, luck won't get you very far if you don't know how to take advantage of it.

It took several chance happenings to make Charles Hires one of the leading soft drink makers. More lucky than good? Not altogether. His lucky breaks were so tiny that the average person might not have taken advantage of them. Hires had the necessary perception and daring to recognize the good fortune that had fallen into his lap.

Charles Hires was born on a farm near Roadstover, New Jersey, in 1851. At the age of 12, he began working at a drugstore in the small town of Bridgeton, New Jersey.

When Hires turned 16, he set out to seek his

fortune in the big city. Arriving in Philadelphia with only 50 cents in his pocket, he talked his way into employment with an established druggist.

Impatient to move on to bigger things, Hires went into business for himself two years later. He borrowed the $3,000 it cost to open his own store.

It must have taken a courageous banker to loan that much money (worth many times $3,000 by today's standards) to an 18-year-old businessman. But Hires paid back the loan almost immediately, thanks to a stroke of luck.

One day Hires was walking past a construction crew digging a cellar for a new building. Unlike most observers at the site, Hires saw that the dirt being dug up and hauled away was a kind of clay known as fuller's earth, which is valuable for filtering and purifying other materials.

Hires offered to take the clay off the crew's hands. He took it home, pressed it, cut it into cakes, and wrapped the cakes in tissue paper to sell. Hires made $6,000 from his lucky find.

That money allowed him to keep his new pharmacy business alive. By 1875 his business was well established and running smoothly. Adding to his festive spirits, he decided to get married that year. Of all his wedding presents, the most useful turned out to be one sent to him by fate.

On their honeymoon, Charles and his wife, Clara, stopped at a country inn. The innkeeper's wife toasted their health with a special family tea. Hires found

By borrowing money from a bank, Hires was making use of credit, an important part of the U.S. business system. **Credit** is the ability to get goods, services, or money in exchange for a promise to pay later. A popular way of describing credit is the saying "Buy now, pay later." Banks play an important role in the credit system. Banks loan, or give, money to businesses and individuals, who must later pay the money back plus **interest**, a payment for the use of the money. Banks, in turn, pay interest to people who place their money in bank accounts.

Charles Hires hoped his root beer would appeal to coal miners.

the brew so delicious that he asked for the recipe. It was a blend of 16 ingredients, including various barks, berries, and wild roots, all steeped in water.

Hires stocked all of the main ingredients — sarsaparilla root, hops, and juniper berries — on his drug shelves. Like most druggists of the time, Hires had been experimenting with his own recipes for medicines. He had always been intrigued by the medicinal value of some of the roots and berries used in the tea.

Convinced that these natural ingredients were healthful, Hires returned home and began to think about the possibility of selling a tea that combined the ingredients.

As a Quaker, Hires was disturbed by people's use of alcoholic beverages — especially the hard-drinking Pennsylvania coal miners. He hoped that "Hires Herb

Charles Hires

Tea," as he called it, would prove so delicious that alcohol consumers would drink it instead of liquor.

Hires Herb Tea was not easy to produce, however. Hires had to enlist the help of two medical school professors to devise a way to make a solid concentrate from the ingredients. Before long Hires was producing little packages of the concentrate. Customers were advised to steep it in water and add sugar and yeast.

A friend of Hires's, the Rev. Dr. Russell Conwell, advised Hires that the rugged coal miners would never drink his product if he called it a tea. If he called it a beer, though, they might give it a try. Hires agreed and changed the name to "root beer."

In 1876 Hires introduced his product to the world at the Philadelphia Centennial Exposition. He offered free samples to the public, and most people responded favorably to the new drink. Hires was able to find customers for his drink besides the coal miners. For the next 14 years, he sold his bright yellow box of solid root beer extract as a sideline to his drugstore business.

It wasn't until 1890 that Hires formed a company to manufacture and sell root beer. But he realized that the new soft drinks being developed, such as Coca-Cola®, were easier to use than root beer, which the consumer had to brew in batches. Hires saved his customers a step by brewing it himself and selling a liquid extract of his product in 1890. Five years later, he took the final step and began bottling ready-to-drink root beer.

Catering to customers' needs by making root beer easier to use was one way Charles Hires marketed his product. **Marketing** is the process of developing a product, determining how much it should cost, deciding how it should be sold, and making sure that people who want to buy the product can get it. One slogan describes marketing as "finding a need and filling it."

Hires was one of the earliest advertisers in the United States. Ironically, like the makers of Coca-Cola, he originally pushed his root beer as a wholesome health drink. But Hires Root Beer sold well because it tasted good, not for its medicinal value.

They Took a Shine to the Wax

Johnson Wax

A basic rule of business involves supply and demand. The number of products that are offered for sale at different prices at a certain time is called **supply**. **Demand** is the number of products that people are willing to buy at different prices at a certain time.

SAMUEL C. JOHNSON, A PROFESSIONAL salesman working in the Midwest in the late 1800s, was so eager to keep customers satisfied that he invested in an attractive small product to include as a gift with his major sales item. The minor product proved so popular that it overshadowed the major product, however. Public demand forced him into a business that he might not have entered otherwise, and he took advantage of his good fortune to build a company whose products fill store shelves in every corner of the United States.

Samuel C. Johnson, born in 1833, worked at many occupations, including sales and railroad work, during his life. Eventually he devoted his time to selling wood products. In the 1880s, he traveled around Wisconsin, selling wood flooring

Samuel C. Johnson launched his parquet flooring business in 1886 at the age of 53. By the time Johnson died in 1919, the company's main product was floor wax.

for a hardware company in Racine, Wisconsin. Johnson was able to save enough money from his commissions to buy the flooring operations of his employer. In 1886, at the age of 53, he was finally running his own business, which he named the S.C. Johnson Company.

Although he was now the boss of a carpentry force of four, he still lived the life of a traveling salesman. Five days a week, he climbed into his horse-drawn buggy and searched for customers. Johnson found enough interest in parquet floors to

A sales **commission** is a fee paid to a salesperson for selling an item. The amount of the commission is usually a percentage of the price of the item sold.

keep his work force busy. Parquet floors—small blocks of wood arranged in artistic patterns—gave rooms an elegant appearance.

Many of Johnson's customers and potential customers expressed concern about how to keep a parquet floor clean. He decided to look into the matter. He bought some floor wax, knowing that wax was commonly used on the floors of European palaces. He gave away a free sample to everyone who bought a floor, and he sold it on the side to customers who needed more.

Before long the floor wax had become a nuisance. The company was spending more time responding to requests for wax than working on its real business, floors. Instead of getting upset by this turn of events, Johnson studied the situation carefully. If he was doing such good business with something he wasn't trying to sell, he could imagine what would happen if he really put effort into it. In 1888 the company placed its first national advertisement—for prepared paste wax. Just two years after he had bought the floor company, Johnson found himself in an entirely new business.

The company continued to make parquet floors until 1917, two years before Samuel's death. By that time, floor wax was the mainstay of the company's business. It was fortunate that the company had found a new business, since parquet floors soon declined in popularity and sales.

The S.C. Johnson Company gradually expanded

An **advertisement** is a way to present ideas, goods, or services to the public. The presentation is paid for by a sponsor, such as Johnson. Johnson's advertisement appeared in a newspaper. Other forms of advertising include television and radio anouncements and billboards.

In the Johnson Wax Company's early days, only a handful of workers (above) were needed. The company's first national newspaper advertisement (far left) appeared in 1888.

Samuel Johnson learned the importance of branching out into new products when the parquet floor business declined in the early 20th century. Many years later, the fourth-generation leader of the company—also named Samuel C. Johnson—faced a similar challenge. In a 1983 interview, he recalled, "My father, who recognized the need for new product because the wax business wasn't growing, told me, 'Sam, it's up to you to find something new.' After a few months, I came up with a proposal for a new product—a Johnson's aerosol insecticide." His idea led to the development of the successful Raid insecticide.

into wood-finishing products, car wax, paints, polishes, and eventually shampoo, insecticides, insect repellents, and a host of specialty chemical products. Presently, more than 11,500 persons owe their jobs to Samuel Johnson's belief in servicing the floors that he sold.

A display of early Wrigley's products

The Prize Became the Product

Wrigley's Gum

WILLIAM WRIGLEY, JR., WAS A GREAT believer in prizes, premiums, and sales gimmicks. He thought that it made customers feel special when he gave them something for nothing. A happy customer was more likely to continue buying his product.

At least twice, though, Wrigley's generous giveaways backfired. Customers paid attention to his prizes but ignored his products. But, like Samuel Johnson, Wrigley kept an open mind. If customers wanted the prize instead of the product, Wrigley made a product out of the prize.

William Wrigley, Jr., was born in 1861, the son of a Philadelphia soap maker. As a child, Wrigley's independent streak troubled his parents. He ran away from home at the age of 11 and ended up in

A **premium** is a gift offered to the consumer (the person who buys a product) as an incentive to buy a specific good—if the customer buys the product, he or she receives a premium. Premiums are not usually related to the product being sold.

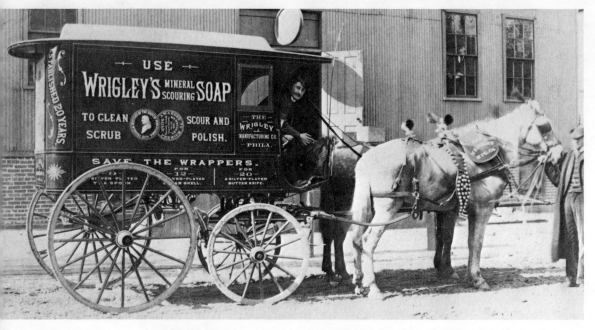

William Wrigley, Jr., got his start in business selling his father's soap.

New York City. There he supported himself for three months by selling newspapers and doing odd jobs. Back home in Philadelphia, he was suspended a number of times from grammar school. After he threw a pie at the nameplate over the school entrance, he was told not to come back.

Wrigley's father decided that hard work would subdue the boy's high spirits. William Wrigley, Sr., gave the 12-year-old the toughest job of all in the soap factory—stirring pots of soap. After standing over the boiling pots with a heavy wooden paddle, William was more than ready to try something else.

The following year, he persuaded his father to let him try his hand at sales. His father sent him off on a wagon pulled by a team of four horses.

For a daring youngster who had already explored New York City on his own, working his own sales territory was a wonderful adventure. As his parents knew, William would not take no for an answer. His first customer had no intention of buying soap, but William followed him around. The boy remained as polite and friendly as he was persistent. Fearing he would never be rid of the boy, the man finally bought the soap. Most potential buyers suffered a similar fate. William even camped overnight on one customer's doorstep in the middle of winter in an effort to make a sale.

Ironically, while Wrigley's reputation as a clever, persistent salesman grew, his bank account did not. After 16 years of selling soap, he hadn't managed to save much money. When he left town to explore the sales situation in Chicago in 1891, he had only $32 to his name.

The soap market in Chicago seemed to hold great possibilities, though, so Wrigley wasn't going to let a meager bank account stop him. Borrowing money to get started, he set up his own sales business. Even though he was still selling his father's soap, he was now in charge of his business, so he was free to try out his promotional ideas. After getting a good price on a supply of baking powder, he gave away a box of the powder free with a purchase of soap.

The **market** for chewing gum or any other product or service means the potential buyers for that product.

The promotion didn't work quite as planned, because customers were more interested in the baking powder than in the soap. Wrigley turned away from his father's soap products and began selling baking powder. Satisfied with his technique of giving away a free prize with a sale, he searched for a new, inexpensive premium. In 1892 he made a deal with the Zeno Manufacturing Company to provide him with chewing gum for a low price. He offered his customers two free pieces of gum with every purchase of baking powder.

Although Native Americans had been chewing a kind of gum made of spruce bark for centuries, packaged gum had only recently been introduced to the United States public. After seeing the famous Mexican general Santa Anna chewing lumps of chicle—a natural gum found in tropical evergreen trees—inventor Thomas Adams had started manufacturing gum in New York in the 1860s. Since then chewing gum had been made in several flavors, but it was still a novelty. Wrigley found that the hidden market for gum was greater than he had dreamed. Before Wrigley, no one had suspected that consumers would be willing to spend millions of dollars per year on such a product.

Just as before, customers lost interest in Wrigley's main product. Many of them wrote to Wrigley asking if they could buy the gum without having to buy the baking powder. Again Wrigley decided to follow the current of customer opinion. If gum

Promotion is all of a company's selling activities, including advertising, face-to-face selling, and special efforts such as coupons or contests. Wrigley's premiums were a form of promotion.

Horse-drawn wagons prepare to leave Wrigley's gum factory. When customers had shown more interest in gum than in baking powder, Wrigley switched to gum production.

was what customers wanted, gum was what they would get.

Certain of his instincts, Wrigley began manufacturing gum. In 1892 he formed the Wrigley Chewing Gum Company. The first brands were called Lotta Gum and Vassar. The following year he added two new flavors, Juicy Fruit and Spearmint.

He knew that anyone could make gum; it was a simple product. The challenge would be to sell it — to make his gum seem better than any other. Fortunately, he could count on the efforts of one of the world's greatest salesmen — himself. Wrigley had lost none of the exuberance of his youth, and he spent most of 1893 knocking on doors. That year he slept in railroad cars on 187 nights. Aiming his premiums at store owners, he offered such items as cash registers and coffee makers to those who stocked large quantities of his gum.

William Wrigley, Jr.

This strategy resulted in gradual growth of the company. But after 15 years in business, Wrigley's gum accounted for just a small portion of the gum sold in the U.S. When the country's economy became depressed in 1907, many businessmen were nervous. Wrigley, however, had never been timid. While his competitors tried to weather the economic downturn by cutting their advertising expenses, Wrigley chose that time to make his big move. Taking advantage of bargain rates from advertising agencies desperate to lure back customers, Wrigley showered the country with ads for his products.

Competition is one of the basic features of the U.S. business system. **Competition** means trying to get something that others are also trying to get. Competition in business can occur in many ways. Producers compete for the best raw materials. Businesses compete with each other for the most customers. Companies compete to make the best-quality or lowest-priced product or service.

His advertising was especially effective because there were few competing ads to confuse the public. At the same time, he continued to give away prizes, such as a free box of gum, to retail store owners who were considering selling his gum. Wrigley also realized that it was not wise to give people a wide choice of flavors, because by doing so he would compete against himself. He eliminated flavors like Blood Orange, Banana, and Sweet 16.

As a result of all his work, Wrigley turned hard times into profitable ones. While other companies were floundering, Wrigley's sales increased 1,000 percent in a single year. By 1910 Spearmint and

Almost 300 women hand-wrap Wrigley's gum in 1901.

William Wrigley Jr. Company headquarters are in the Wrigley Building on Michigan Avenue in Chicago, Illinois.

Juicy Fruit ranked first and second in sales among all gum sold nationwide.

The master salesman did not stop there, however. Five years later, he collected every phone directory he could. Wrigley mailed four free sticks of gum to each of the 1.5 million subscribers in those books. With boundless energy (he arose at 5:00 A.M. every day and never took a vacation unless it was business-related), Wrigley continued to promote his products until his death in 1932.

All he had intended to do was sell soap. But by being alert to an opportunity, Wrigley turned a sales gimmick into a successful product and made his business one of the most recognized companies in the United States.

The Forgotten Dough

Kellogg's Corn Flakes

Young Will Keith Kellogg as a broom salesman

WILL KEITH KELLOGG'S FAMILY believed that it would take more than a stroke of good luck to launch him on his way to business success. It would take a miracle.

They were wrong. After more than 40 years of humiliation suffered at the hands of his own family, Will Keith (W.K.) made his name a centerpiece on breakfast tables throughout the United States.

There could hardly have been a less likely candidate for fame and fortune than W.K. Kellogg. Born in 1860 in Battle Creek, Michigan, W.K. seemed both socially and intellectually backward. The boy had few friends and, by all appearances, no outstanding talent. He was labeled a "slow learner" by his parents, and they pulled him out of school at the age of 13. His brother, John Harvey, was eight years older. John Harvey excelled in his studies and went on to become a famous surgeon, while W.K. worked in his father's broom factory.

In 1880 John Harvey offered W.K. a job at the Battle Creek Sanitarium, where John Harvey was superintendent. Dr. Kellogg had already earned a national reputation with his books on health and nutrition. He had gone on to turn the Sanitarium into one of the most prestigious health care facilities in the country.

W.K. was given a job as business manager, but the title was more impressive than the work. For the next 25 years, W.K. was little more than a glorified servant of his older brother. He ran errands, performed handyman jobs, did bookkeeping, and worked as a shipping clerk and cashier. Although John Harvey was a millionaire thanks to the lucrative sanitarium business, the doctor paid his brother meager wages. The most money W.K. ever made at the Sanitarium was $87 per month. Stories even circulated around Battle Creek that W.K.'s jobs included shaving John Harvey and shining his shoes. W.K. began to refer to himself as "John Harvey's flunky." As much as he resented the way his brother treated him, W.K. remained dependent on his brother for work.

Dr. John Harvey Kellogg

Dr. Kellogg put patients at the Sanitarium on a rigid diet. Much like health food regimens today, the emphasis was on eating grains, fruits, and vegetables and on avoiding sugar. The doctor

The Battle Creek Sanitarium as it appeared in the late 19th century. Part health resort, part hospital, part spa, the Sanitarium attracted many wealthy and famous clients.

required that food be easy to digest. While experimenting with methods of making an easily digestible wheat bread, the Kelloggs came up with a new breakfast cereal that was also easy to digest.

The Kelloggs tried to avoid the mushy texture of most cooked cereals. After boiling grain into a doughy consistency, they ran it through rollers which pressed the dough into thin sheets. The sheets were baked and then crumbled into pieces. Always trying to improve his products, Dr. Kellogg had W.K. experiment with the process to get the best results.

One day in 1896, W.K. made an accidental discovery. The previous day he had been called away from his last batch of boiled grain. Instead of being run directly through the rollers, as usual, it had been left to sit all night. The next morning, W.K. ran the dough through the presses anyway, with an unexpected result. Instead of sticking together in sheets as usual, the wheat broke into flakes. The overnight waiting time had allowed moisture to saturate each of the individual wheat berries. This caused them to separate rather than cling together when pressed.

Dr. Kellogg viewed the disaster and suggested that the flakes be toasted and then ground up. But W.K. decided to toast them and serve them just as they were. Compliments from Sanitarium patients encouraged him to investigate the flaking process more closely. Before long he had come up with a tasty barley flake and an oat flake. Corn didn't seem to work as well until W.K. switched from whole kernel corn to corn grits.

Sanitarium residents enjoyed the corn flakes. In 1898 the doctor received so many requests from former Sanitarium residents who wanted corn flakes that he agreed to ship out some of the cereal.

The loyalty of these people to corn flakes convinced W.K. that there could be a great public demand for the product. He tried to persuade his brother to sell corn flakes to grocery stores. Every time he brought it up, however, John Harvey dismissed the idea. The doctor did not want to tarnish his professional reputation by stooping to commercial sales. For the next eight years, the flakes were sold strictly as a mail-order item to former clients.

W.K. Kellogg

Kellogg experimented with different kinds of grains to develop his corn cereal. In a more formal process called **research and development**, many companies conduct experiments to create new products or improve existing products. **Research** is investigation aimed at discovering new scientific knowledge. **Development** is the attempt to use new knowledge to make useful products or processes.

A product is said to be **commercial** if it is sold for money.

Finally, in 1906, at the age of 46, the so-called "slow learner" broke away from his famous brother. Buying out John Harvey's share of the cereal patents, he went into business for himself, forming the Battle Creek Toasted Corn Flake Company.

Free from his brother's rigid control, W.K. Kellogg put his own stamp on the product. He altered the recipe so that it would appeal to more than a handful of health food dieters by adding small amounts of sugar, salt, and malt to improve the taste.

W.K. Kellogg's first product was Toasted Corn Flakes. Kellogg's signature appeared on the box.

At the same time, W.K. proved he wasn't the dullard his family had thought. Though shy and uncomfortable in social situations, he showed no timidity in promoting his product. His aggressive, catchy ads and astute business sense helped to put corn flakes in grocery stores across the country. Business increased so quickly that W.K. was able to shrug off a devastating fire in 1907 and use it as an excuse to build a new, larger plant.

In 1922 W.K. changed the name of his business to the Kellogg Company. Kellogg's Corn Flakes® became the best-selling breakfast cereal in the United States, and the company began making other kinds of cereals as well. "John Harvey's flunky" had created a familiar part of the modern breakfast table. It might not have happened were it not for a forgotten batch of dough.

A **patent** is the exclusive right to own, use, and dispose of an invention. Since Dr. Kellogg owned the cereal patents, W.K. Kellogg had to buy the patents before he could start making and selling the cereal on his own. Anyone who invents a machine, device, or process can apply for a patent. The U.S. Patent Office issues more than 1,200 patents each week.

Kellogg Company headquarters are located in Battle Creek, Michigan.

A Candy Bar Named After Whom?

Baby Ruth

Baseball slugger Reggie Jackson could hardly be accused of thinking small in his career goals. Most Valuable Player Awards and World Series rings might have been enough for most players, but not even induction into baseball's select Hall of Fame could satisfy him. At the peak of his career, Jackson announced that what he really wanted was a candy bar named after him.

It was no mystery what Reggie was talking about. The "Baby Ruth" candy bar had been one of the United States' most popular snack items for more than 50 years. Like most people, Jackson figured it must have been named after Babe Ruth. No other player in sports history had inspired a candy bar.

There was only one flaw in Jackson's quest for a personal candy bar: Babe Ruth never had a candy bar named after him! According to its inventor, the Baby Ruth bar was named after someone much less famous.

No one can judge exactly how this case of mistaken identity affected the fortunes of the Curtiss Candy Company, the original maker of the Baby Ruth bar. But the fact that nearly everyone who has ever heard of a Baby Ruth assumes it is Babe Ruth's namesake indicates that the name was a lucky coincidence. Companies often spend thousands of dollars on advertising so that consumers will recognize the names of their products. The wave of publicity that the Yankee star stirred up helped the candy bar achieve instant name recognition.

The man behind this lucky candy bar was Otto Schnering, the son of an immigrant jeweler. Born in Chicago in 1891, he attended the University of Chicago. Following his graduation in 1913, he worked for several years as a retail sales manager for a piano company.

In late 1916, he decided to seek his fortune making candy. After purchasing some secondhand candy-making machinery, he opened his business in a small room above a Chicago plumbing shop. With one experienced candy-maker and three assistants to help him, Schnering began testing recipes in his five-gallon kettle.

Five years later, he perfected a blend of caramel, fudge, peanuts, and chocolate, which he sold in five-cent bars. Local customers bought his new

Publicity is news that is not paid for about ideas, products, people, or institutions. Even though Babe Ruth had nothing to do with the Baby Ruth candy bar, he was featured in newspaper stories and unwittingly provided publicity for the candy. In a sense, publicity is "free advertising."

For a new product to be successful, customers must be made to want the product. An important part of that process is getting customers familiar with the name of the product. That is what is meant by **name recognition**.

candy bars as fast as he could make them. Schnering moved to larger quarters and he had to hire 125 people to keep up with demand.

Luck alone did not account for Schnering's success. Besides having skill as a confectioner, he knew how to promote his product. And he was aware of the importance of names.

From the beginning Schnering understood the effect of names on the public. He used his mother's maiden name, rather than his own name, when he formed the Curtiss Candy Company. His reasons for not using his own name have not been recorded, but shortly before Schnering started his company, the United States was on the verge of a war with Germany. Consumers might not have responded favorably to an obviously German name like Schnering. The choice of the name Curtiss was prudent.

Schnering foresaw problems with the name of his most popular product, the nut bar that he had dubbed "Kandy Kake." Although the bar was extremely popular, competition from other companies was growing fierce. Schnering thought that an uninspiring name like Kandy Kake would not hold the public's attention. In 1921 he asked for suggestions from his employees for a better name for the bar. The winning submission was "Baby Ruth," after the eldest daughter of former president Grover Cleveland.

This explanation may sound a bit farfetched today.

Otto Schnering

After all, how many people have ever heard of Ruth Cleveland? Moreover, Grover Cleveland had left the White House 25 years before Schnering named his bar. George Herman "Babe" Ruth, meanwhile, had just rocked the sports world by achieving an astounding total of 54 home runs in 1920, more than twice as many as any other player had ever hit in a season. Babe Ruth's colorful exploits made fascinating reading even for those who were not sports fans. Otto Schnering no doubt knew all about the New York Yankee, since the candy-maker was an avid baseball fan.

In 1930, when Babe took steps to make his own "Babe Ruth" candy bar, Schnering took Ruth to court. Babe Ruth backed down. The Yankees were just beginning to solidify into a winning team, and neither they nor Babe had yet attained the mystical aura that later surrounded them.

Baby Ruth Cleveland, on the other hand, had been a very popular girl. She was born in 1891, just before her father was elected to his second term as president. The toddler romping through the White House charmed the public. The warm glow cast by the little girl was cut off when Ruth died of diphtheria at the age of 12.

At the Columbian Exposition of 1893, an engraved medal depicting President Cleveland and his wife with their baby, Ruth, was displayed. Since the Exposition was held in his hometown, Schnering was quite familiar with it. So when the employee

Opposite: President Grover Cleveland with wife Frances and daughter Ruth as depicted in the early 1890s

New York Yankee Babe Ruth, one of the greatest and most famous baseball players of all time, hit 714 home runs in his career. His fame helped promote the Baby Ruth candy bar.

named the candy bar "Baby Ruth," Schnering thought the name was a good choice.

Schnering spared little effort in calling attention to his product. He hired a 26-plane aerial circus to drop thousands of free candy bars attached to tiny parachutes over 40 major cities. In Pittsburgh, Pennsylvania, the bars floated down at rush hour and were blamed for causing a traffic jam.

While this deliberate promotion helped sell Baby Ruth bars, the Yankee player Babe Ruth was also unintentionally boosting the product. Six years after the Baby Ruth bar was unveiled, Babe Ruth hit 60 home runs in a season, a record that stood for more than 30 years. Ruth's record of 714 home runs in his career lasted even longer. Not only did he become one of the most famous baseball players ever, but his memory was kept alive over time when youth baseball leagues were referred to as Babe Ruth leagues.

Because of Babe's fame, it is little wonder that the Curtiss Company's candy bar became associated with him. Other manufacturers spent millions of dollars to get endorsements from celebrities so that people would remember their products. Without hiring a celebrity, the Curtiss Company had found one of the most memorable names of all time.

The Answer Was Right Under Their Noses

Kleenex Tissue

KLEENEX® IS SUCH A COMMONLY USED name that many people don't know that it is a brand name. Only the facial tissue made by Kimberly-Clark Corporation is a Kleenex tissue. Most people know how a Kleenex tissue is used. Surprisingly, when the product was introduced, its own manufacturer did not know what Kleenex tissue was good for. They were selling the right product for the wrong reason. Only after practical consumers pointed out to Kimberly-Clark that the tissue was perfect to blow one's nose on did Kleenex tissue become a major product.

The company was started with a bit of loose talk from a paper-mill employee in the early 1870s. While lounging with some friends in a club in Neenah, Wisconsin, the man revealed how much money his employer made from his paper mill. The figures he cited caught the attention of a number of people in the club, including John Kimberly and Charles Clark.

Kimberly had moved to Neenah from Troy, New York, in 1848. After two years of operating a general store, he had decided to take advantage of the water power made available by the rapid drop of the Fox River near Neenah. Like other enterprising businessmen, Kimberly had built a flour mill. Then he heard from the paper-mill employee that the money he was making grinding grain was hardly worth the effort compared to the potential of a paper mill.

Charles Clark, another ex-New Yorker, perked up his ears at this news as well. A veteran of the Civil War, he hadn't found his niche in the business world since leaving the service. A paper mill sounded like a venture worth exploring. In 1872 Kimberly and Clark, along with two other investors, formed a company to manufacture paper. Kimberly agreed to oversee sales while Clark supervised the mill. The two men hired the talkative employee who had first interested them in paper mills as plant foreman.

The company's first product was newsprint, which was made from old linen and cotton rags. The plant had barely begun turning out its high-quality paper when the country was hit by the Panic of 1873. The panic occurred when investors became nervous about the possibility of banks closing and withdrew their money from them. The sudden loss of money forced

Investing money in a business means giving money or something else of value to the business with the expectation of getting the money back with a little extra if the business is successful. Every new business requires an initial investment of some amount of money. It may be the money of the person starting the business, as in Kimberly's and Clark's case, money from a group of investors, or a loan from a friend or a bank.

Charles Clark

John Kimberly

some banks to go out of business. Other banks collected the money they had lent to businesses.

Not only did Kimberly and Clark weather the crisis, but they were able to buy companies that did not survive the panic. In 1878 they took over a new mill in nearby Appleton. The new mill produced wrapping paper from groundwood pulp. Showing an ability to adapt and recover from setbacks, the company continued to expand. When a fire devastated their newsprint mill, they converted their wrapping-paper mill machines to newsprint. Newsprint was back in production within four weeks.

During the company's long period of growth, Kimberly-Clark management kept an eye out for new wood-pulp products and processes. When word came from Europe of a new paper product that could absorb liquid better than cotton did, the company sent people overseas to investigate. They scarcely had begun studying this fluffy product when World War I broke out and forced them to return to the safety of the United States.

They had learned enough, however, to manufacture a similar wadding material, which the company called Cellucotton®, also a Kimberly-Clark brand name. The product proved valuable when the United States entered World War I in 1917. As supplies of cotton dwindled, hospitals and first aid stations turned to Kimberly-Clark's Cellucotton material as a substitute. Toward the end of the war, a stronger version of the material was also used as a gas-mask filter.

To satisfy the war demand, Kimberly-Clark's plants churned out reams of the tissue paper. At the end of the war, however, the company found itself stuck with warehouses full of a product that was no longer needed.

In searching for a new use for the product, Kimberly-Clark took stock of the mood of the

The word **production** refers to all activities involved in converting natural resources, such as iron or trees, into finished goods, such as plows or wood or paper. The word **manufacturing** refers to the making of articles by hand or with machines.

*Production of Cellucotton peaked during World War I. After the war,
the Kimberly-Clark Corporation sought new uses for the material.*

country. People seemed to want to put the terrible war behind them and focus on happier, more glamorous things. Kimberly-Clark decided to steer its product as far away from the memories of war and hospitals as it could.

Removing Cold Cream

as Beauty Experts Urge

To Correct a Grave Mistake in Skin Care

NOW REDUCED IN PRICE

Due to volume production, the price of Kleenex 'Kerchiefs has been greatly reduced. With 30% more 'Kerchiefs in each box as well, the present price of Kleenex is scarcely more than half what you paid before.

230 LARGE HANDKERCHIEF SHEETS...50c
(Big size—90 sq. in. each)

PLEASE ACCEPT a 7-day supply of this NEW and utterly different way to try

Makes cleansing creams 4 to 6 times more effective.

Holds your make-up fresh hours longer than before.

Corrects oily skin and nose conditions amazingly.

SPECIALLY POSED FOR KLEENEX 'KERCHIEFS BY IRENE RICH, CHARMING WARNER BROS. STAR

Ends
—Oily skin and nose conditions amazingly.
—The expense of ruining and laundering towels.

Keeps
—Make-up fresh hours longer than before.
—Lightens skin several shades—quickly.

NOW it has been discovered that by removing cleansing cream *thoroughly* from your skin, the cleansing power of cold cream can be multiplied from *four to six times.*

That's because it has been learned that towels, cloths, etc., being insufficiently absorbent, largely rub the dirt back in, and thus foster many skin disorders.

To meet that condition, a new and utterly different way of removing cleansing cream has been developed. Results on your skin will amaze you. Send the coupon and a 7-day supply will be sent you.

Virtually every beauty authority urges this new way. Scarcely a star of stage or screen but who employs it. It is far cheaper to use than 'spoiling and laundering towels. Women by the thousands are flocking to its use.

Ends two beauty mistakes

It ends the soiled towel method, judged dangerous to skin beauty. Too often you *thus rub dirty cold cream back into the skin.* That fosters skin blemishes. It invites blackheads. It is a prime cause of oily skin and nose conditions. To use cold cream effectively, you must remove

it *all* from the skin. Towels, cotton cloths, paper substitutes, won't do it.

It ends, too, the mistaken use of too harsh paper makeshifts; not sufficiently absorbent to thoroughly cleanse, too harsh for delicate skin fabric.

End those mistakes, and you'll note an amazing difference *quickly* in your skin. Your make-up will hold hours longer than before. Your skin will lose its oily look. Your nose will seldom call for powder.

Send coupon

A few days' use will prove the results of the Kleenex 'Kerchief beyond all question or doubt. Mail the coupon. A full 7-day supply will be sent you.

For COLDS

Never Again Use Handkerchiefs

They Re-infect—Spread Germ Contagion

LARGELY on medical advice, thousands now use Kleenex 'Kerchiefs for colds. *For thus one discards at once the excretions that spread—that re-infect as well.*

Soiled, damp handkerchiefs are bad. They carry possible contagion—*re-infection*—with you. Remember this when you or your children have a cold.

Damp handkerchiefs, too, tend to chap and irritate the nostrils. Kleenex 'Kerchiefs are dry, fully absorbent and fresh every time you use them. Thus no chapping or skin irritation. You discard like paper. Next cold, try them.

KLEENEX
ABSORBENT
'KERCHIEFS
To Remove Cold Cream—Sanitary

Kleenex 'Kerchiefs—absorbent— come in exquisite flat handkerchief boxes to fit your dressing table drawer. Professional size: Sheets 9 x 10 inches . . 50c

Promoting the product as an easy, disposable way of cleaning off makeup, the company called it "KLEENEX." Kimberly-Clark's "Sanitary Cold Cream Remover" was introduced in 1924 as a substitute for

At first, Kleenex tissue was mar-keted as a way to remove makeup and cold cream (left). *Later, after surveys revealed that most people used Kleenex to blow their noses, the product was advertised as useful for colds* (right).

face towels, and the brand name KLEENEX was registered as a trademark. To reinforce a glamorous image, the company sought and received endorsements from Hollywood movie stars.

At a price of 50 to 65 cents for a 100-sheet carton, Kleenex tissue sold only moderately well in spite of the celebrity plugs. But it did prompt an occasional letter from a blunt consumer. "Why don't you ever say it's good for blowing your nose?" read a typical query.

After hearing this comment many times over the years, the company conducted a survey in 1930 to find out how its customers were using Kleenex tissue. They found that the attempt to sell the product as a facial-cleansing tissue had missed the mark. Kleenex tissue was selling only because most consumers had found their own use for it. More than 60 percent of those surveyed reported that they were using the tissue as a disposable handkerchief.

Following the customers' lead, Kimberly-Clark revamped its advertising. It was as if a switch had been turned on. Sales of Kleenex tissue doubled within one year of its being sold as a throwaway hanky and then doubled again the following year. Within six years, the success of Kleenex tissue had helped boost Kimberly-Clark's work force from about 2,800 employees to more than 4,000. Not only did Kleenex tissue become a household necessity, it also helped pioneer a generation of disposable paper

The word *Kleenex* is a trademark. A **trademark** is a distinctive, legally protected symbol, title, or design used by a company to distinguish its products from those of other companies. Many companies spend a lot of money protecting their trademarks. Sometimes, however, a trademarked word is used so widely that it becomes a generic word. For example, nylon, aspirin, and thermos were once brand names.

Surveys are a common way to perform marketing research. **Marketing research** is done to find out what people want and the best way to satisfy their needs. **Surveys** are groups of questions that researchers ask a lot of people in order to gather their views and opinions.

products, including napkins, plates, towels, and diapers. It had been Kimberly-Clark's good fortune to miss its target, only to hit a much more profitable one accidentally.

The Accident With 40,000 Uses

Owens-Corning

Fiberglass can be used to make a remarkably diverse range of products, from boats (above left) to firemen's helmets (below left) to chairs (above).

THE CONCEPT OF SURVIVAL OF THE fittest applies not only to the natural world; it is a basic principle of competitive business as well. Enterprises that cannot adapt to a changing world are doomed to fail. Products and companies that are better able to satisfy the consumer will take their places. In the 1930s, United States glassmakers began to wonder if their businesses could survive.

Glass had many desirable characteristics to offer consumers: it didn't burn, rot, rust, or stretch; it could withstand acid; it was waterproof, transparent, and could be molded into many shapes. But all of these features could not make up for a major flaw: glass was fragile. Because it broke and shattered so easily, it was unsuitable for most purposes. While new uses were found for durable substances such as metal, rubber, and, eventually, plastic, it seemed that glass had limited use. It always performed the same functions: as bottles, windows, test tubes, dishes, drinking glasses, and decorative items.

The future of the glass industry appeared so uncertain that two large glass companies independently undertook major research efforts in the 1930s. Unknown to each other, both the Owens-Illinois Glass Company of Ohio and the Corning Glass Works of New York set up laboratories to explore other possible uses for glass.

Owens-Illinois began their effort by hiring a consultant named Games Slayter. While touring the company's bottle-making plant, Slayter lingered at the glass-melting furnace. There was an opening in the furnace into which raw materials such as sand and soda ash were fed to be melted. Just outside this hole, Slayter discovered a small pile of glass which had formed into long fibers. The intense heat coming from the furnace had melted some of the glass before it entered the furnace. The air pressure caused by the heat had pulled the glass into fibers. Normally the stringy glass was thrown away, but Slayter suggested studying it for possible practical use.

Slayter was far from the first person to discover glass fibers. Thousands of years ago, the Egyptians had made glass fibers for use in decorating bottles and other glassware. But no one had tested these

The glass **industry** refers to the group of glass manufacturers as a whole. The word *industry* can also be used more generally to mean all of a nation's manufacturing activity.

Games Slayter

A gob of molten glass can be stretched by hand into long, string-like fibers.

In general, an economic **depression** is a period when production and consumption of goods and services slow down. It is a time marked by unemployment and business failures, and people do not have much money to live on. During the 1930s, the United States suffered through a period called the **Great Depression**, during which the U.S. economy was paralyzed.

fibers to see what their characteristics were, nor did anyone know how to produce them rapidly in large quantities.

Owens-Illinois then swam against the stream of a devastating economic depression by setting up a small research laboratory in its Evansville, Indiana, factory. Progress was difficult at first, because researchers did not know how to make the fibers easily. The only known process for making fibrous glass was to heat a batch of raw material and stretch it by hand into long strings. The longer the glass could be kept hot, the longer and finer the fibers could be. The end product, however, was rarely as delicate as desired; one researcher said working with it was "like massaging a porcupine."

At the same time, the company's interest in

producing new glass products led to the development of ways to make heavy blocks of glass. The blocks could be used by the construction industry for durable basement windows or as decorative bricks. These blocks were made in two halves and then fused together.

While experimenting with ways of fusing these halves, the Owens-Illinois researchers used a metal air gun. Ordinarily, metal was fed into the gun, where it met a hot flame. The melted metal was blown out in the form of tiny liquid beads by a strong blast of air. These beads acted as a "glue" which fused pieces of metal when they cooled and solidified.

Researchers hoped they could use glass in the same manner to weld the glass blocks together. At first they poured powdered glass into the gun, but the process failed. Then the scientists tried feeding rods of glass into the gun, as in traditional metal welding. Instead of shooting out beads of molten glass, however, the glass was blown out in long, hair-like fibers.

The technician using the gun tried making adjustments, but everything he tried ended up as a stringy mess on the floor. He was discouraged and perhaps a little embarrassed by the mess until a lab manager looked closely at what had happened. The technician had stumbled upon a new, economical way to make glass fibers. The use of forced air made large-scale production of the material possible.

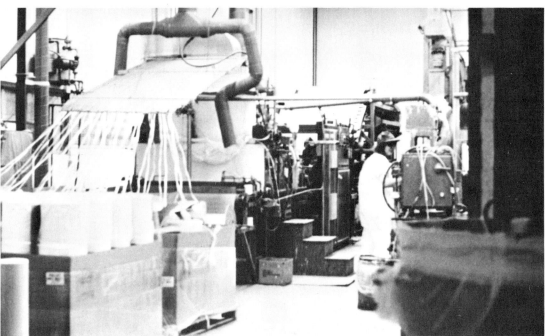

As part of the process of molding fiberglass into an object, a worker directs a stream of chopped fiberglass into a rotating screen (above). *On another machine, fiberglass is chopped into short strands* (below).

Air filters for furnaces and air conditioners were the first commercial products made of fiberglass.

Now that they knew how to make glass fibers, researchers faced another exciting challenge: What kinds of products could be made from this untapped resource? Testing showed that fiberglass was far more versatile than ordinary glass. Unlike ordinary glass, fiberglass was strong, soft, and even bendable. At the same time, it had all of the valuable traits of regular glass.

The first commercial use discovered for the new product was in air filters for furnaces and air conditioners. Owens-Illinois began marketing its handy, inexpensive, lightweight, fiberglass air filter in 1932. It worked so well that it has remained the standard forced-air furnace filter to this day.

Corning had also been investigating glass fibers. When Owens-Illinois and Corning Glass Works discovered that both companies were researching

The Chevrolet Corvette—introduced by General Motors in 1953 as a "dream car"—was the first automobile built with a fiberglass body. To demonstrate the frame's light weight, a GM worker holds it above his head.

new markets for fiberglass, they decided to pool their knowledge and resources. In 1938 the two companies formed a new company, the Owens-Corning Fiberglas Corporation. The trademarked name for their new product was *fiberglas*. (The generic name for the product is *fiberglass*.) Over the years, the number of uses for fiberglass has multiplied, with no end in sight. Fiberglass is used in many products, including building insulation, automobile tires, space suits, storage tanks, fishing poles, and boats.

Benton's Gift That Keeps on Giving

Encyclopaedia Britannica

Encyclopaedia Britannica headquarters in Chicago

WILLIAM BENTON WAS NOT OBSESSED with wealth or big business. At the height of a successful career in advertising, he decided he had made enough money and retired at the age of 35. But whether he wanted to or not, Benton would continue to be successful in business. For the rest of Benton's life, his instincts and keen business skills combined to make him a wealthy man.

Benton was born in Minneapolis, Minnesota, in 1900. His father, a language professor at the University of Minnesota, died when William was in his early teens. The Benton family was left to struggle financially, but Benton was awarded a scholarship to Yale University.

After graduating in 1921, Benton sold cash registers for a short time before seeking his fortune in New

An astute businessman, Benton led Encyclopaedia Britannica for 30 years. He later became a senator.

York City. There he accepted a job with an advertising agency. Benton proved adept at this work and by 1925 he was put in charge of all the copywriters at the Lord & Thomas Agency. He then hired an assistant, Chester Bowles, who quickly became one of his closest friends. The two men often talked of starting their own advertising agency and, in July of 1929, they put their plan into action.

The country entered the Depression just months after Benton and Bowles opened shop, and the two men worked feverishly to keep their tiny business afloat. They assured nervous clients that it was

A business with two or more owners, or partners, like the advertising firm that Benton and Bowles started, is called a **partnership**. A business owned by just one person is called a **sole proprietorship**. Large companies with many owners are called **corporations**. Although the corporation has become the major form of business in the U.S.—providing the most jobs and generating the most income—most businesses are still sole proprietorships.

more important than ever to advertise during those tough economic times. Their firm earned a reputation as resourceful and daring.

By 1935 the agency had become so profitable that the 35-year-old Benton decided he had made as much money as he needed. He decided to sell his share of the business.

Because of his modest life-style, Benton did not need all of his money. As a favor to a friend, he invested $5,000 in a foundering shoe company. The company recovered so vigorously that within 10 years Benton's small investment was worth $125,000.

A few years later, Benton bought a company called Muzak, which recorded tapes of continuous, soothing music and sold them to hotels, dentists' offices, banks, and other places. When he sold Muzak 20 years later, he made over $4 million from his $132,500 investment.

Benton's success continued with Encyclopædia Britannica. Encyclopædia Britannica had been started in 1768 by three men in Edinburgh, Scotland. More than a century later, some United States businessmen bought the encylopedia. In 1920 the company ended up in the hands of the giant mail-order and department store firm, Sears Roebuck & Company. By the early 1940s, Sears executives were beginning to lose interest in Encyclopædia Britannica. Sales were not outstanding, and some critics charged that the publication was "long-winded and dull."

An 18th century caricature depicts two of the men who founded the Encyclopaedia Britannica: Andrew Bell (left), engraver and publisher, and William Smellie, editor.

The first edition of Encyclopaedia Britannica was published in 1768; it was issued in 100 parts, each installment appearing every other week or so. The first edition was full of both scholarly and practical information, such as a cure for toothache ("laxatives of manna and cassia dissolved in whey") and a method to make counterfeit emeralds.

Benton had become a vice president of the University of Chicago in 1937, and now he had an idea that would benefit both Sears and the University of Chicago. In 1941 he met with General Robert E. Wood, head of Sears. Benton showed Sears how it could give away its encyclopedia and save, not lose, money. He suggested that Sears make a gift of the publication to the University of Chicago. As Benton pointed out, gifts to the university were tax-deductible.

Wood was convinced. Sears offered to give the Encyclopaedia Britannica to the university Board of Trustees twice, first in 1941 and again in late 1942. The second offer was particularly generous. But the trustees were reluctant to spend the thousands of dollars it would cost to run Britannica's operations. It was an offer the university could not afford to accept.

Not wanting to see the university lose a golden chance, Benton agreed to ease the university's financial burden by investing $100,000 of his own money in the encyclopedia. An arrangement was made in which the University of Chicago acquired one-third of the stock and Benton the other two-thirds. Benton also agreed to take on the responsibility of running the company himself.

Benton was not as interested in making money as he was in watching the University of Chicago keep the old encyclopedia alive. "It's the only business I have ever dealt with that will still be going 100 years from now," he said, explaining his involvement. He wanted to help the cause of education, one of his passionate interests.

As chairman and publisher, he guided Encyclopaedia Britannica through three decades. Relying on his experience in advertising, Benton used radio and television to advertise the product. He also improved the sales system.

Sales skyrocketed under Benton's direction. The slow growth pattern of more than 180 years was

By investing a large amount of money into Encyclopaedia Britannica, Benton was buying shares, or portions, of stock in the company. A **stock** is a small part of ownership in a company. Ownership is usually divided among many shareholders or owners. Stocks are traded—bought and sold—in stock exchanges. The most famous stock exchange is on Wall Street in New York City.

Today the Encyclopaedia Britannica is sold in more than 100 countries. The encyclopedia is so well known that the company receives about 2,500 pieces of mail each day.

forgotten. The value of the company increased along with its sales. Investment analysts noted that a share of ownership in Encyclopaedia Britannica was worth several times what it had been a few years earlier.

During this time, Benton's career broadened beyond the university and the encyclopedia. He served as assistant secretary of state under President Harry S Truman and later became a U.S. senator representing Connecticut.

Benton had taken a 175-year-old tradition and built it into a robust company. By the time of his death in 1973, Benton was a rich man, and the University of Chicago had reaped millions of dollars in royalties from sales of the encyclopedia. By trying to help the University of Chicago, Benton had amassed a fortune.

For Further Reading...

Bryant, K.L., Jr. and Dethloff, H.C. *A History of American Business*. Prentice-Hall Inc., 1983.

Clary, D.C. *Great American Brands*. Fairchild Books, 1981.

Fucini, J.J. and Fucini, S. *Entrepreneurs: The Men and Women Behind Famous Brand Names*. G.K. Hall, 1985.

Livesay, H.C. *American Made: Men Who Shaped the American Economy*. Little, Brown & Company, 1980.

Moskowitz, M., Katz, M. and Levering, R., eds. *Everybody's Business*. Harper and Row, 1980.

Slappey, S.G. *Pioneers of American Business*. Grosset & Dunlap, 1970.

Sobel, R. and Sicilia, D.B. *The Entrepreneurs: An American Adventure*. Houghton Mifflin Company, 1986

Thompson, J. *The Very Rich Book*. William Morrow & Company, 1981.

Vare, E. and Ptacek, G. *Mothers of Invention: From the Bra to the Bomb: Forgotten Women and Their Unforgettable Ideas*. William Morrow & Company, 1988.

INDEX

Words in **boldface** are defined in the text.

Schnering, Otto, 40-45
S.C. Johnson Company, 20-23
Sears Roebuck & Company, 67-70
Slayter, Games, 58
Smellie, William, 68
Smith, Carl, 10
sole proprietorship, definition of, 67
stock, definition of, 70
supply, definition of, 19
survey, definition of, 54

T

Toasted Corn Flakes, 37
trademark, definition of, 54
Truman, Harry S, 71

U

University of Chicago, 69-71
University of Minnesota, 65

W

Wall Street, 70
William Wrigley Jr. Company, 24-32
Wood, General Robert E., 69
World War I, 50-51
Wrigley Building, 32
Wrigley Chewing Gum Company, 30
Wrigley, Jr., William, 25-32
Wrigley's gum, 11, 24-32

Y

Yale University, 65

Z

Zeno Manufacturing Company, 28

John Kimberly and Charles Clark took over the Atlas paper mill, which produced wrapping paper, in 1878.

ACKNOWLEDGEMENTS

The photographs and illustrations in this book are reproduced through the courtesy of: pp. 1, 12, 16, 17, The Procter & Gamble Company; pp. 2, 18, 20, 22, 23, S.C. Johnson & Son, Inc.; pp. 8, 15, 43, The Library of Congress; p. 10, General Mills, Inc. Archives; p. 11, George S. Bolster; pp. 24, 26, 29, 30, 31, 32, Wm. Wrigley Jr. Company; pp. 33, 34, 35, 36, 37, Kellogg Company; p. 41, Planters LifeSavers Company; p. 44, National Baseball Library, Cooperstown, New York; pp. 46, 49, 51, 52, 53, 55, 76, Kimberly-Clark Corporation; pp. 56, 57, 61, Molded Fiber Glass Company; pp. 58, 62, Owens-Corning Fiberglas® Corporation; p. 59, The Department of Archives and Records Management, Corning Glass Works; p. 63, General Motors; pp. 65, 66, 68, 69, 71, Encyclopaedia Britannica, Inc.

Cover illustration by Stephen Clement.